AMERICA'S SUPERNATURAL SECRETS ™

ALIEN SIGHTINGS IN AMERICA

Jennifer Bringle

rosen publishing's
rosen
central

NEW YORK

To Rodney, my favorite UFO believer

Published in 2012 by The Rosen Publishing Group, Inc.
29 East 21st Street, New York, NY 10010

Library of Congress Cataloging-in-Publication Data

Bringle, Jennifer.
Alien sightings in America/Jennifer Bringle. — 1st ed.
    p. cm. — (America's supernatural secrets)
Includes bibliographical references and index.
ISBN 978-1-4488-5530-8 (library binding)—
ISBN 978-1-4488-5578-0 (pbk.)—
ISBN 978-1-4488-5579-7 (6-pack)
1. Unidentified flying objects—Sightings and encounters—United States—Juvenile literature. I. Title.
TL789.2.B75 2012
001.942—dc23

2011017354

Manufactured in the United States of America

CPSIA Compliance Information: Batch #W12YA: For further information, contact Rosen Publishing, New York, New York, at 1-800-237-9932.

Contents

Introduction

Be it in movies, in books, or even on the news, UFOs (unidentified flying objects) have become a major part of popular culture in the United States. Flying saucers and large-eyed aliens are everywhere from T-shirts to Halloween costumes to toys. UFO and alien sightings have been the subject of curiosity and debate for centuries, and interest in them has only grown in the past few years.

Even before the invention of airplanes, people in America have reported seeing strange aircraft in the sky. As early as 1878, UFO sightings were recorded in the United States, and these sightings continued throughout the years, reaching a fever pitch during World War II and the years following the war. Many cases, such as the Roswell Incident in New Mexico in 1947, the Betty and Barney Hill abduction in 1961, and the Phoenix Lights in 1997, have heightened the interest in UFOs. New sightings happen frequently, even though most of them go unreported.

While many sightings can be explained away, there are a few that defy explanation. These are the cases that continue to interest many people and prompt continuing investigation. They've also inspired countless books, movies, and television shows, such as *Fire in the Sky* and *UFO Hunters*. And as pop culture embraces UFO phenomenon, it's clear these mysterious aircraft will continue to be a subject of interest.

Aliens have become a major part of popular culture. They are portrayed in books, movies, television shows, and even Halloween costumes. Every Halloween, aliens walk the streets in droves.

Chapter 1

Early Sightings

Many people think that UFO sightings are an occurrence that has only happened during the last century. That's not true. Even years before human beings took to the sky in airplanes and other flying craft, sightings of strange things in the sky began to pop up.

What Are UFOs?

Popular culture generally depicts UFOs as flying saucers carrying aliens. But that's not reality. UFO stands for "unidentified flying object." Unidentified flying objects are any unusual object or phenomena in the sky that cannot be readily identified. In most cases, UFOs are ordinary objects, such as weather balloons, meteors, or military aircraft, which are mistaken for something unidentifiable by observers. A small number of UFOs are hoaxes—fakeries created by people to fool others. And in even fewer cases, UFOs are indeed unexplainable aircraft or other objects.

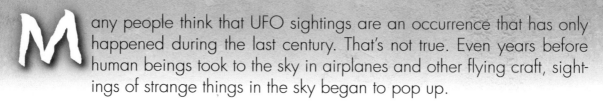

Weather balloons, which are used to help monitor and forecast weather conditions in the sky, are often mistaken for UFOs. They are one of the top explanations for UFO sightings.

7

While the flying saucer shape is the most commonly known form of UFO, the craft are seen in a variety of shapes:

- Flying saucer—This shape looks like an upside-down saucer, or bowl.

- Spherical—This ship is shaped like a sphere, or ball.

- Triangular—This UFO is shaped like a triangle, or sometimes like a V.

- Cylindrical—A cylinder-shaped craft looks like a giant cigar.

- Dirigible—This shape is rounded with pointed ends, like the Goodyear Blimp.

- Ellipsoidal—This shape looks like an oval or egg.

Just as shapes vary in UFOs, so do other characteristics. Many have lights, which can vary by color, shape, and whether or not they blink. UFOs have also often been described as having a metallic look. Their movement also varies. Some ships are described as fast-moving, zipping through the sky at speeds rarely seen in normal aircraft. Others are said to move slowly or hover over the ground. Another common description of UFO movement is a combination of both, where a craft hovers or moves slowly and then takes off at a rapid speed. Also, most UFOs do not make sound as regular aircraft do. And often, reports of electromagnetic interference (meaning magnetic fields are disturbed, causing lights to flicker, appliances to malfunction, etc.) on the ground are reported at the time of UFO sightings.

UFO sightings have been reported around the world. While some of these sightings are unexplained, many can be attributed to ordinary phenomena. Common objects mistaken for UFOs are:

- Airplanes, helicopters, balloons, and other ordinary aircraft

- Meteors, planets, or other naturally occurring astronomical phenomena

Many UFO sightings, including some of the earliest recorded sightings, have been over farmland and other rural, lesser-populated areas and small towns.

- Weather balloons, blimps, and other meteorological equipment
- Birds, insects, or other animals

Early Sightings in America

While it may seem that UFO sightings are a modern phenomenon, the truth is that sightings were reported as far back as the 1800s. One of the earliest was reported on January 25, 1878, in Denison, Texas. A farmer named John Martin reported seeing a large, dark, circular object flying through the air at a rapid speed. In a story in the *Denison Daily News*, Martin described the craft

Flying Saucers: Fact or Fiction?

In movies and on television, UFOs are most often depicted as flying saucers. Many actual reports of UFOs describe the same thing. But is there an explanation for what these people are seeing? There are several theories/explanations for flying saucers:

- Lenticular clouds—These clouds take on a disk shape.
- Balloons—There are many balloons, some used for weather forecasting, that have a saucerlike shape.
- Fata Morgana—This is a type of mirage, or naturally occurring optical phenomenon, in which light rays are bent to produce a displaced image of distant objects or the sky. The Fata Morgana effect can distort the image of ordinary objects to both the naked eye and radar.
- Hoaxes—Many photos and videos of flying saucers are fakes created by people to fool others.

as being the size and shape of a saucer. This was the first known use of the word "saucer" in association with a UFO sighting.

Nearly three decades later, on February 28, 1904, three crew members on the USS *Supply*, a U.S. Navy ship stationed 300 miles (483 kilometers) west of San Francisco, reported seeing unidentified flying craft over the ocean. Lieutenant Frank Schofield, who was on the ship, reported that the sailors saw three bright red, egg-shaped and circular objects in the sky. The objects were flying in echelon formation, a military flying formation in which aircraft fly in a diagonal line. The objects then changed course and flew above the clouds and out of sight.

What made the Denison and USS *Supply* sightings so significant is the fact that there were no airplanes flying in the air at that time. The Wright brothers made the first human-driven airplane flight in 1903, and it took many years for airplanes to develop for travel over the ocean. There were balloons and other nonpowered aircraft at the time, but they did not resemble the shapes described in these sightings.

During the 1920s, as airplanes became more common, UFO sightings picked up again. This time, they were seen by fellow aircraft in the air. In January 1926, a pilot reported seeing what he described as "flying manhole covers" traveling between Wichita, Kansas, and Colorado Springs, Colorado. Just a few months later, in September, an airmail pilot flying over Nevada was forced to land after being bombarded by a large, wingless, cylindrical object. In both these cases, no explanation was ever found.

chapter 2

Wartime/Postwar Sightings

During World War II, many Americans watched the sky with fear and anxiety. The possibility of air attacks, such as the one on Hawaii's Pearl Harbor, were a real threat. But during that time, military planes weren't the only aircraft seen in the sky. Many people, including pilots and military personnel, reported seeing unidentified objects in the sky during the World War II years and in the years immediately following.

Wartime Sightings

In February 1942, just months after the attack on Pearl Harbor, people in Los Angeles were on edge. The city's size and proximity to Japan made it a prime target for a military attack. Military forces, as well as civilians, were on high alert.

On the nights of February 24 and 25 in 1942, air raid sirens rang out in Los Angeles. As was procedure during air raids, a blackout of the entire city

During World War II, air raid sirens sounded in Los Angeles during a sighting that was later dubbed "The Battle of Los Angeles." Many thought UFOs were to blame, and the incident inspired a 2010 film.

WORLD INVASION:
BATTLE LOS ANGELES

COLUMBIA PICTURES PRESENTS IN ASSOCIATION WITH RELATIVITY MEDIA AN ORIGINAL FILM PRODUCTION BATTLE: LOS ANGELES AARON ECKHART MICHELLE RODRIGUEZ RAMON RODRIGUEZ BRIDGET MOYNAHAN NE-YO AND MICHAEL PEÑA MUSIC BY BRIAN TYLER COSTUMES BY SANJA MILKOVIC HAYS EDITOR CHRISTIAN WAGNER PRODUCED BY PETER WENHAM DIRECTOR OF PHOTOGRAPHY LUKAS ETTLIN EXECUTIVE PRODUCERS JEFFREY CHERNOV DAVID GREENBLATT ORIGINAL FILM WRITTEN BY CHRIS BERTOLINI PRODUCED BY NEAL H. MORITZ ORI MARMUR DIRECTED BY JONATHAN LIEBESMAN WORLDINVASIONBATTLELA.NET SONY COLUMBIA PICTURES

COMING SOON

13

was called, meaning everyone had to turn off their lights to make it harder for aircraft to see targets on the ground. The sirens were sounded because of reports of unidentified blinking lights and flares in the sky. Fearing an attack from the Japanese military, the 37th Coast Artillery Brigade began firing anti-aircraft shells into the air. They fired shots for nearly an hour, with approximately 1,400 shells being fired.

Just hours after the air raid ended, Secretary of the Navy Frank Knox held a press conference. In it, he dismissed the whole incident as a false alarm, blaming it on paranoia and anxiety over the war. But many local residents and members of the press did not believe the incident to be just a false alarm. A number of theories began to circulate—from Japanese submarines stationed offshore with the capability to transport aircraft, to a hoax perpetrated by coastal defense industries in an attempt to move their operations farther inland. Another theory that has endured to the present day is that the mysterious lights were alien aircraft. Since they weren't officially identified at the time, the craft do technically fit the description of UFOs. However, many theorists went even further, suspecting the military of covering up the incident because the craft was alien in nature. This, of course, has never been proved, but it's still a popular theory among UFO believers. In 1983, the Office of Air Force History concluded that after analysis of all available evidence in the case, the mysterious craft were weather balloons.

Postwar Sightings

During the years after the end of World War II, the reports of UFO sightings began to increase. Several of the most important and highly publicized UFO cases occurred during these years. One of those was the Kenneth Arnold sighting.

Kenneth Arnold's account of a UFO sighting near Mount Rainier in Washington State became a sensation and stands as one of the most memorable, and still unexplained, sightings of the twentieth century.

The Flying Saucer as I
Saw it... by Kenneth Arnold
Per copy 50¢

In June 1947, businessman Kenneth Arnold was flying his private plane near Mount Rainier, Washington, when he spotted something strange in the sky. He saw a line of nine, shiny, disk-shaped crafts traveling at extremely high speeds along the face of the mountain. He described the objects as being very thin, and one of them was crescent-shaped, while the others were more disklike.

When Arnold landed his plane in Yakima, Washington, later that day, he told his friend, who was also the airport's general manager, what he'd seen. Soon, word of the sighting began to spread. The next day, he was interviewed by the *East Oregonian* newspaper in Pendleton, Oregon. After that, Arnold received a large amount of publicity that ranged from interviews with the Associated Press to receiving countless letters from people who thought he was crazy. Once his story came out, several others came forward to say they'd seen similar objects flying near Mount Rainier at the same time that Arnold did. Additionally, many other sightings were reported across the country in the wake of Arnold's report, including a very similar sighting by the crew of a United Airlines flight en route from Idaho to Seattle.

In July 1947, the U.S. Air Force opened an investigation into Arnold's claims. After interviewing Arnold and determining that he was credible, they ruled that what he'd seen was a mirage. Shortly thereafter, the Federal Bureau of Investigation (FBI) began investigating some of the UFO sightings—including Arnold's and the one by the United Airlines crew. Their findings determined that these reports were not adequately explained by the military's findings and that these people actually saw something flying around. These findings led to another investigation, which resulted in the formation of Project Sign at the end of 1947, the first publicly acknowledged U.S. Air Force UFO investigation. Project Sign eventually became Project Grudge and then evolved into the better-known Project Blue Book.

Another famous UFO incident occurred in 1947, in Roswell, New Mexico. That July, the Roswell Army Air Field reported that staff from the field's 509th Bomb Group recovered a flying disk that crashed near a ranch outside Roswell. This news became a sensation with the media, and reports filled newspapers and radio about the crash of a flying saucer. Shortly thereafter,

Major Jesse Marcel poses with some of the debris found near Roswell Army Air Field in Roswell, New Mexico. Many believe the debris is from a crashed UFO, while the army denies those reports.

the commanding general of the Eighth Air Force said that it was a radar-tracking balloon, not a flying disk, that was found by the base's personnel. In a press conference called by officials at the base, the media were shown debris from the crashed object. The debris looked to have come from a weather balloon and not a flying saucer.

After the military explanation was given, the case very rarely mentioned for many years. But in 1978, a physicist and UFO investigator, Stanton T. Friedman, reignited interest in the Roswell Incident. He interviewed Major Jesse Marcel, who helped with the recovery of debris from the crash in 1947. Marcel told Friedman that he believed the military may have created a

Stanton Friedman, UFO Expert

While nuclear physicist Stanton Friedman became famous for his study of the Roswell UFO incident, he has had a long, successful career as a scientist.

Stanton was born in 1934 in New Brunswick, Canada. He studied nuclear physics at the University of Chicago and received his bachelor's degree in 1955 and his master's in 1956. For more than a decade, he worked as a nuclear physicist for companies such as General Electric, General Motors, and McDonnell Douglas. During this time, he worked on nuclear aircraft and rockets, giving him the experience to comment on UFOs.

During the late 1950s, Friedman got interested in UFOs and began studying many of the major cases. He became a popular lecturer on the subject, traveling around the United States and Canada speaking on the topic. His interest and expertise on the topic of UFOs led him to interview Major Jesse Marcel, who was involved with the recovery of debris from the Roswell crash. This investigation thrust him into the national spotlight, leading him to write the book *Crash at Corona: The Definitive Study of the Roswell Incident.*

cover-up, and the debris may have actually come from an alien spaceship. His story became popular with UFO believers, and eventually the *National Enquirer* interviewed Marcel on the subject. After Marcel's statements were made public, others began to come forward, claiming knowledge of or involvement with the incident. One in particular, a mortician named Glenn Dennis, said he conducted autopsies on the bodies of dead aliens pulled from the wreckage.

After these new revelations, a congressional inquiry was made, followed by an inquiry by the Government Accountability Office (GAO). It asked the Office of the Secretary of the Air Force to conduct an internal investigation. The findings were released in two reports. The first report was released in 1995, and it said that the debris was probably from a secret government program called Project Mogul. Project Mogul used high-altitude balloons to pick up sound waves from Soviet atomic bomb tests and missiles. The second report was released in 1997 and dismissed reports of alien bodies. It concluded that these reports were either hoaxes or people confusing or mis-remembering the bodies of servicemen and/or anthropomorphic (describing nonliving objects with human proportions or characteristics) dummies used in military test programs as alien bodies.

The UFO believer community disregarded these findings as improbable and another attempt to cover up the crash of an alien spaceship. To this day, the town of Roswell is commonly related to the phenomena of UFOs and aliens. This characterization has become something the town has embraced and used to draw tourists.

In response to the rash of UFO sightings in 1947, the U.S. military, specifically the air force, began investigating the evidence of UFOs. Beginning in 1947, a long-term investigation called Project Blue Book began (although it was called Project Sign and then Project Grudge until 1952). The project had two major goals: to determine if UFOs were a threat to national security and to scientifically analyze UFO-related data.

During the years that the project was in effect, the military compiled thousands of reports of UFO sightings. The investigation reports were submitted by both military personnel and civilians. The reports were analyzed and filed, and the air force requested help from the University of Colorado. The Condon Committee, the informal name of the University of Colorado UFO Project was led by physicist Edward Condon from 1966 to 1968. After studying hundreds of files from Project Blue Book, the committee chose fifty-six to further evaluate.

The final report, formally titled "Scientific Study of Unidentified Flying Objects," but commonly called the Condon Report, was published in 1968. The report concluded that studying UFOs probably would not produce any major scientific discoveries. However, it said that some cases should be investigated, primarily those involving credible people with good ideas. The committee noted that there were gaps in scientific knowledge in the fields of "atmospheric optics, including radio wave propagation, and of atmospheric electricity" that might benefit from further research in the UFO field. The report concluded that there was nothing out of the ordinary about UFOs. The report was reviewed by a panel of the National Academy of Sciences, which approved its conclusions. However, there were others, including investigators who worked on the project, who questioned its methodology and bias.

As a result of the Condon Report, the air force shut down Project Blue Book in 1969. The air force summarized its conclusions based on both investigations during Project Blue Book and the findings of the Condon Report:

- No UFO reported, investigated, or evaluated by the air force was ever a threat to national security.

- There was no evidence submitted to or discovered by the air force that UFO sightings represented technological developments beyond the range of modern human scientific knowledge.

- There was no evidence indicating that sightings categorized as UFOs were alien vehicles.

Another major investigation into UFO activity was the Brookings Report, which was commissioned by the National Aeronautics and Space Administration

(NASA) in 1960. The investigation, officially called "Proposed Studies on the Implications of Peaceful Space Activities for Human Affairs," was created by the Brookings Institution (a nonprofit public policy organization), in collaboration with NASA's Committee on Long Range Studies.

The report discusses the need for research on issues related to space exploration, but it also includes passages on the implications of a discovery of extraterrestrial life. The report does not specifically recommend a government cover-up of evidence of extraterrestrial life, but it does mention this as a possibility. The section discusses possible public reaction to the discovery of alien life-forms and makes the case for further research of UFOs and the possibility of extraterrestrial life. It suggests a need for research on possible public reactions and how this kind of event could impact society. Due to that, the report has been repeatedly cited by the UFO believer community as evidence that cover-ups did occur. The report was submitted to the Committee on Science and Astronautics of the U.S. House of Representatives in 1961.

Later that year, another major UFO-related event occurred that made history. A couple from New Hampshire, Barney and Betty Hill, reported that they were abducted by aliens. The couple, who were respected citizens of their community, were returning home from a vacation on September 19, 1961. As they drove down a nearly deserted road, they saw a bright light in the sky. Thinking it was a satellite, they pulled over to take a look. Barney got out binoculars and took a closer look. When he did, he claimed he saw a craft with rows of multicolored lights and windows with beings standing inside them. Still, he thought it was possibly a military aircraft of some sort, since they were near Pease Air Force Base.

As they continued to travel down the road, the craft grew closer and seemed to be following them. They watched as it rapidly descended right above their car. They said they could easily see the humanlike beings inside, watching them. Terrified, they drove off quickly, but then their car stalled and began vibrating, and they reported entering an almost sleeplike state, with their bodies tingling.

The Hills finally made it home at dawn, unable to fully remember the events that occurred the night before. They examined themselves and noticed

Barney and Betty Hill claimed that they were abducted by a UFO in 1961. The two experienced memory loss and nightmares that led them to try hypnosis to find out what really happened to them.

strange damage to their clothes and belongings, such as tears on Betty's dress and a rip on Barney's binoculars strap. Shortly after the event, Betty contacted Pease Air Force Base to report the incident. The Hills were then interviewed by air force officials, and they concluded that the couple had mistaken the planet Jupiter for a spacecraft. The report was included in Project Blue Book.

Within two weeks of the encounter, Betty began having vivid nightmares about being abducted by aliens. In her dreams, they conducted medical examinations and experiments on her and her husband. She was so troubled by the dreams that she and Barney began investigating hypnotherapy to either relieve her of the dreams or try to recover their lost memories from that night. The two kept their experience mostly private until a newspaper article was published in 1965 that detailed their account. Other stories followed and brought the couple international attention. They eventually wrote a book about the experience, along with writer John G. Fuller and their hypnotherapist, Dr. Benjamin Simon. The book was called *The Interrupted Journey*. In 1975, their story was also brought to television in a movie called *The UFO Incident*.

Chapter 3

Aliens in the Modern Age

While UFO sightings reached a fever pitch during World War II and the two decades following, the modern era has also seen a large number of sightings and other incidents. But due to advances in technology, the number of hoaxes has also increased, as people are more and more capable of creating realistic fakes. Still, there are many cases from the past few decades that defy explanation.

Sightings in the 1970s and 1980s

During the 1970s, several major UFO incidents occurred, creating more interest in UFOs than ever. One of the most publicized of these events was the alleged abduction of Travis Walton by an alien spacecraft. His story inspired the movie *Fire in the Sky*.

In November 1975, Walton was working as a logger with a crew in the Apache-Sitgreaves National Forest in Arizona. On the evening of November 5, Walton and his crew had finished their work for the day, and they got into a truck to head back to Snowflake, Arizona, where they lived. As they were driving down the road, they saw a bright light shining beyond a hill ahead of them. When they got closer to the hill, they saw a large, brightly lit, metallic disk hovering over a clearing. The driver stopped driving once he saw the

In 1975, Travis Walton claimed he was abducted by a UFO near Apache-Sitgreaves National Forest in Arizona. The incident inspired the movie *Fire in the Sky*.

disk. At that point, Walton jumped from the truck and ran toward the strange craft. The other men yelled at him to stop and come back, but he ignored them and ran to the UFO.

Once Walton reached the craft, it began making a loud noise, and then started to tilt from side to side. At that point, Walton began slowly backing away from the disk. But just as he started to move away from the craft, his coworkers said a beam of light shone down from the disk right onto Walton. They watched him being lifted into the air into the light, and then he was thrown back down onto the ground, nearly 10 feet (3 m) away. His boss, who was driving the truck, panicked and drove away, thinking Walton was dead and that the UFO would come after them, too.

The crew drove about a quarter of a mile (.4 km) away and then decided to go back and check on Walton. When they returned, the disk was gone, and so was Walton. They searched for about a half hour for him and then left. When they got into town, they called the police, and Deputy Sheriff Chuck Ellison met with members of the crew. They told him what happened, and some of the men cried as they told their story. Shortly thereafter, a massive search began, with the help of volunteers, police and even helicopters. Word began to spread about what happened, and national media came to the town to cover the unbelievable story.

Despite days of intense searching, Walton was not found. During that time, his coworkers were all interviewed again and given lie detector tests. Police were suspicious of their story, and wanted to determine if they'd killed him and lied to cover it up. The tests concluded that the men were telling the truth. Also during this time, several people began to say that the whole thing was a hoax, and that Walton and his brother Duane and tricked his coworkers. No firm evidence of this was ever found.

On November 10, five days after he'd disappeared, Walton called his brother-in-law and told him he was at a gas station in a nearby town. When his brother-in-law picked him up, he noticed that Walton was clearly very upset and afraid. Once he got home, he had a hard time eating without vomiting. And though his family tried to keep it quiet that he'd returned, the media found out about Walton's reappearance. After he began to feel better, Walton told the story of being abducted by aliens. He said they performed medical examinations and experiments on him. Walton said he met with several human-like beings who put a gas mask on his face, making him pass out. When he awoke, he was back in Arizona.

Walton's story garnered a great deal of media attention. It was also met with a great deal of skepticism from those who did not believe in UFOs or aliens, such as journalist Philip J. Klass. In 1978, Walton published an account of his story, called *The Walton Experience*. That same year, another book, *The*

Former president Jimmy Carter admitted that he saw something strange in the sky over Georgia. While he classified it as a UFO, he said he did not think it was an alien spacecraft.

Ultimate Encounter, was written by Bill Barry, who argued against those who did not believe Walton. In 1993, Walton's book was adapted into the movie, *Fire in the Sky*, which starred D. B. Sweeney as Walton.

In 1976, UFOs were in the news again, this time because of Jimmy Carter, who was running for president at the time. He told the story of seeing a UFO in the sky over Leary, Georgia, in 1969. Carter was standing outside at night when he noticed a bright light along the horizon. The light began to move closer to where he was, getting brighter and brighter. Carter said it also changed colors, from white to blue to red and back to white. Several other people also witnessed the light.

Carter reported his sighting to the International UFO Bureau in 1973. He said he thought the object he saw was a UFO, but he did not believe it was an alien spacecraft. Some have said that Carter merely mistook the planet Venus, which was at maximum brightness that night, for a UFO. The sighting has never been officially explained.

During the 1980s, a significant and extended period of sightings began in the Hudson River Valley region of New York. Starting in 1982, and lasting through 1995, more than seven thousand sightings were reported in the skies above New York and Connecticut. Witnesses reported seeing brightly lit, boomerang-shaped crafts moving silently through the sky. The first sighting was observed by a retired policeman in Kent, New York. He reported seeing the boomerang-shaped craft that was seen countless times over the next decade. Another sighting during this time occurred in 1984 near the Indian Point nuclear reactor complex on the banks of the Hudson River. Witnesses saw a strange flying object hovering over one of the nuclear reactors. It then flew toward the river and then sped off.

In 1986, the crew of Japanese Airlines flight 1628 saw three unidentified objects flying over Alaska. The cargo plane was flying toward Anchorage en route to Tokyo when the captain reported seeing three UFOs. The largest was shaped like a shelled walnut, and all three were traveling at about the same speed as the plane. They continued following the plane, and even veered toward it at one point. Military radar picked up the objects trailing the

In 1997, many people reported seeing strange lights in the sky over Phoenix. The incident, dubbed the "Phoenix Lights," was later mocked by Arizona's governor during a press conference.

plane and the Federal Aviation Administration (FAA) requested military intervention. The military did not take any action, however, and the objects stopped following the plane. The FAA investigated the incident but could not explain it.

Sightings During the 1990s to the Present

During the 1990s, UFO sightings continued to occur in the United States. One of the most widely publicized was the Phoenix Lights. On March 13, 1997, thousands of people across Nevada and Arizona reported seeing a strange,

The Ed Walters Hoax

One of the biggest UFO sightings of the 1980s also ended up being one of the biggest fakes. In November 1987, Gulf Breeze, Florida, resident Ed Walters reported a series of UFO sightings over a period of three weeks. He said he saw UFOs flying in the air above his home and that he even saw an alien standing outside his back door. He claimed to have taken photos of the flying craft, which proved to be unusually clear and easy-to-see for UFO photos. The photos generated a great deal of excitement, both from the UFO community and the media. But upon further investigation by UFO researcher Jerry Black, the photos' legitimacy came into question. Black discovered a suspicious money trail leading to Walters, which led him to believe the photos were a hoax. Over the years, more suspicion was raised when new evidence was found. In 1990, after the Walters family moved, the new residents discovered a model of a UFO poorly hidden in the attic that bore a strong resemblance to the craft in Walters's photographs. While some still believe Walters, his reports and photos are generally considered to be nothing more than fakery crafted to gain attention and money.

lighted craft flying through the night sky. Witnesses reported seeing two distinct events involved in the incident: a triangular formation of lights seen throughout Arizona and a series of stationary lights seen in the Phoenix area. Many witnesses said the lights appeared to be attached to a massive V-shaped craft.

The first report of the lights and craft came in from Nevada. Shortly thereafter, they were seen in several towns in Arizona. They were also reported by several witnesses in the area around Prescott, Arizona. The sightings hit a fever pitch in Phoenix. Many reported seeing lights in a triangle formation hovering over the city for more than two hours. They were photographed and videotaped and received a great deal of media attention.

The incident was explained away as military flares, or tricks of the eye, but many believe the lights were from an alien spacecraft.

Another mass sighting occurred from August 2004 to October 2006 in the Chicago suburbs of Tinley Park and Oak Park. During the five sightings, two in 2004, one in 2005, and one in 2006, witnesses reported seeing three silent, lighted objects that were red or red-orange in color and spherical in shape, hanging in the night sky and moving slowly in formation for about thirty minutes in each occurrence. The objects in each event were at low to intermediate altitude and were visible from the ground for approximately 12 miles (19 km) in any direction.

Because of their odd lights and flight characteristics, many believe they were not conventional aircraft. The sightings received a great deal of press but were never investigated by the FAA or any other governmental agency. Their origin is still unknown.

Another sighting in the Chicago area came in 2006, when people at Chicago O'Hare International Airport reported seeing a saucer-shaped UFO in the sky near the airport. Several airport workers saw the object hovering over one of the airport's gates. They called the authorities, but later the FAA dismissed the claim as a misidentified weather phenomena.

Chapter 4

Aliens in Pop Culture

Alien and UFO sightings have captured the interest and imagination of human beings for years. So it's no wonder that many books, films, and television shows have featured storylines involving aliens and UFOs. While some of these are total works of fiction, there are some that are based on true events.

Aliens in Books and on the Radio

One of the first and most famous appearances of aliens in pop culture was the H. G. Wells novel *The War of the Worlds*. Published in 1898, it tells the story of an unnamed narrator navigating the suburbs of London while the city is under siege by Martian invaders. Broken into two parts, the book details the alien invasion and the war between humans and aliens once the Martians have taken over. It is the earliest story that details a conflict between aliens and mankind.

Wells's book inspired a 1938 Halloween radio drama as part of the "Mercury Theatre on the Air" series. Directed and narrated by Orson Welles, the performance featured several "news bulletins" warning of the alien invasion. Due to the realistic sound of the bulletins, many listeners were confused and thought the world was actually under attack by aliens. Public panic was

One of the first interpretations of aliens in popular culture was Orson Welles's radio show *The War of the Worlds*, based on H. G. Wells's novel. Many mistook the show as reality and panicked that aliens were invading.

followed by widespread outcry against the show. Even though many were outraged, the show helped make Welles a star.

Another popular book about aliens was written by alien abduction victim Travis Walton. *The Walton Experience* was published in 1978 and tells the

In 1979, Sigourney Weaver starred in *Alien*, a thriller about a bloodthirsty alien trying to kill the crew of a space station. The film became a huge success and spawned several sequels.

story of Walton's abduction, in his own words. The book inspired the movie *Fire in the Sky*.

Aliens in Film

For many years, aliens and flying saucers were a mainstay in B-movies. But in 1977, aliens became blockbuster movie fare with the production of *Close Encounters of the Third Kind*. Written and directed by Steven Spielberg, the film starred Richard Dreyfuss as a man whose life changes after he has an experience with a UFO. The film was a success, becoming one of the first alien films to become a beloved classic.

Two years later, Ridley Scott directed *Alien*, which starred Sigourney Weaver as Ellen Ripley, a warrant officer working on a commercial spaceship. While traveling through space, the ship is attacked by alien creatures that attempt to kill everyone on board. The aliens in this film were some of the

E.T. Makes Aliens Friendly

In most movies and television shows, aliens were depicted as scary creatures. That changed when Steven Spielberg revisited the subject of aliens with 1982's *E.T.: The Extra Terrestrial*. This film was significant because it didn't portray aliens as scary or even dangerous. Starring Drew Barrymore and Henry Thomas, the movie tells the story of a lonely boy who befriends an alien accidentally left on Earth. The boy tries to keep E.T. a secret from his mother, as well as the government, which wants to study him. E.T., the alien, is kind and becomes the boy's friend.

Because of this softer portrayal, *E.T.* was a huge success with both kids and adults. It became one of the most popular movies of the 1980s and was rereleased several times. The movie also spawned all kinds of products for kids, from E.T. stuffed animals to T-shirts and bedding. To this day, it remains one of the most beloved family movies of all time.

most monstrous ever portrayed in movies. And in part because of their horrifying look, the film won an Oscar for Best Visual Effects. The film was a huge success and thus spawned several sequels, including *Aliens* in 1986, *Alien 3* in 1992, and *Alien Resurrection* in 1997.

Independence Day was released on July 2, 1996, and starred Will Smith. Based loosely on H. G. Wells's *The War of the Worlds*, the film tells the story of an alien attack on Earth that takes place on July 4, America's Independence Day. The next year, Will Smith starred in another alien-focused film, *Men in Black*. Tommy Lee Jones and Smith portrayed agents in a secret agency that monitored alien activity on Earth. The story was partially based on the pop culture/UFO conspiracy theorist belief in men dressed in black suits that hassle UFO witnesses to keep them quiet. The film did not really portray them in this negative light.

During the 1990s, *The X-Files* became a huge television success telling the story of two FBI agents investigating cases involving paranormal activity. The series, which starred David Duchovny and Gillian Anderson, also spawned several feature films.

Aliens on Television

Aliens have been a popular theme in television. During the 1980s, the mini-series and television series *V* told the story of aliens living in spaceships, hovering over major U.S. cities. The show was resurrected for a television series by ABC in 2009.

Several other alien-focused shows, such as *Alien Nation*, followed the original *V*, but aliens didn't become a major force in television until 1993, when *The X-Files* debuted. The show, starring David Duchovny as FBI agent Fox Mulder and Gillian Anderson as FBI agent Dana Scully, told the story of two agents who investigated unsolved cases involving paranormal activity. Agent Mulder was portrayed as an alien believer, while Scully was a skeptic. Their cases often involved aliens and UFO encounters. Though fiction, the show was very popular among UFO believers because it helped spark interest in UFO phenomena. It stayed on the air until 2002 and spawned two films.

Recently, the interest in UFOs and aliens has grown more popular. With that interest have come several reality shows on the History Channel. *UFO Hunters* debuted in 2008 and features William J. Birnes, the publisher of *UFO Magazine*. Along with a team of scientists and investigators, Birnes investigates UFO and alien sighting reports. They analyze photos, videos, and other reports, as well as famous cases.

Also on the History Channel, the show *Ancient Aliens* explores claims that aliens visited ancient cultures and helped them make some of the developments of their time. The success of programs like these shows that the interest in UFOs and aliens remains strong among people in the United States. Until we can explain all these events, that interest will continue to grow.

Glossary

abduction The act of being carried away by force; kidnapping.

aeronautic Pertaining to the design, construction, and navigation of aircraft.

aerospace The atmosphere and outer space considered as a whole.

alien A common name for a being not of this planet.

anthropomorphic Nonliving objects with human proportions or characteristics.

autopsy A postdeath examination of a body, including the internal organs.

ballistic missile A missile that is guided in the first part of its flight but falls freely as it approaches its target.

bias Influenced in an unfair way.

bulletin A brief notice from an authoritative source; a news report.

conventional Normal or usual.

cylindrical Having the shape or qualities of a cylinder.

dirigible An airship or blimp, such as the Goodyear Blimp.

ellipsoidal Shaped like an oval or egg.

extraterrestrial Originating, located, or occurring outside Earth or its atmosphere.

Fata Morgana A type of mirage, or naturally occurring optical phenomenon, in which light rays are bent to produce a displaced image of distant objects or the sky. The Fata Morgana effect can distort the image of ordinary objects to both the naked eye and radar.

Federal Aviation Administration (FAA) The branch of the U.S. Department of Transportation that monitors and regulates air travel.

hoax Something that is fake or unreal, created by a person to fool others.

lenticular clouds Clouds that take on a disk shape and could possibly be mistaken for a UFO.

meteor A small particle of matter that can be seen from Earth as it burns up upon entering the atmosphere.

methodology The principles and procedures of a study.

National Aeronautics and Space Administration (NASA) The government agency in charge of the United States' space program; it conducts aerospace and aeronautical research.

phenomenon An exceptional or unusual event or thing.

skeptic Someone who habitually doubts accepted beliefs.

spherical Shaped like a sphere or ball.

unidentified flying object (UFO) An object observed moving through the sky that cannot be conclusively explained.

For More Information

Brookings Institute
1775 Massachusetts Avenue NW
Washington, DC 20036
(202) 797-6000
Web site: http://www.brookings.edu
The Brookings Institute is a nonprofit public policy organization that conducts independent research on a variety of topics. It has investigated and researched UFO sightings and reports throughout the years and produced the Brookings Report.

Center for UFO Studies (CUFOS)
P.O. Box 31335
Chicago, IL 60631
(773) 271-3611
Web site: http://www.cufos.org
CUFOS is an international group of scientists, academics, investigators, and volunteers dedicated to the continuing examination and analysis of the UFO phenomenon.

Federal Aviation Administration (FAA)
800 Independence Avenue SW
Washington, DC 20591
(866) 835-5322
Web site: http://www.faa.gov
The FAA regulates the airways of the United States. It is often called upon to investigate cases of UFO activity.

Fund for UFO Research
P.O. Box 7501
Alexandria, VA 22307
Web site: http://www.ufoscience.org
The Fund for UFO Research works to support all reasonable and scientific
efforts to learn the nature of UFO phenomena.

Mutual UFO Network (MUFON)
2619 11th Street Road, Suite 21
Greeley, CO 80634
(888) 817-2220
Web site: http://www.mufon.com
MUFON works to promote scientific research of UFO activity and keeps a
database of reports and evidence for research purposes.

National Aeronautics and Space Administration (NASA)
Suite 5K39
Washington, DC 20546-0001
(202) 358-0001
Web site: http://www.nasa.gov
NASA works to explore and research planets, galaxies, and other aspects
of space.

Transport Canada
330 Sparks Street
Ottawa, ON K1A 0N5
Canada
(866) 995-9737
Web site: http://www.tc.gc.ca
Transport Canada regulates the airways of Canada. It also investigates
some UFO reports in Canada.

UFO*BC
9271 Barnes Road
Delta, BC V4C 4V2
Canada
(866) 878-6511
Web site: http://www.ufobc.ca
UFO*BC is a nonprofit group that gathers and investigates UFO sighting
reports in British Columbia and the Yukon.

Web Sites

Due to the changing nature of Internet links, Rosen Publishing has developed
an online list of Web sites related to the subject of this book. This site is
updated regularly. Please use this link to access the list:

http://www.rosenlinks.com/amss/alie

For Further Reading

Alexander, John B. *UFOs: Myths, Conspiracies, and Realities*. New York, NY: Thomas Dunne Books, 2011.

Anaya, Rudolfo. *Chupacabra and the Roswell UFO*. Albuquerque, NM: University of New Mexico Press, 2008.

Burgan, Michael. *Searching for Aliens, UFOs, and Men in Black (Unexplained Phenomena)*. Mankato, MN: Capstone Press, 2011.

Dennett, Rosemary. *UFOs and Aliens* (Mysteries, Legends, and Unexplained Phenomena). New York, NY: Checkmark Books, 2008.

Duncan, John. *UFOs* (Unexplained Series). Costa Mesa, CA: Saddleback Educational Publishing, 2009.

Evans, Christopher. *Aliens & UFOs*. Glasgow, Scotland: Carlton Books, 2009.

Friedman, Stanton T. *Captured! The Betty and Barney Hill UFO Experience: The True Story of the World's First Documented Alien Abduction*. Pompton Plains, NJ: New Page Books, 2007.

Friedman, Stanton T. *Flying Saucers and Science: A Scientist Investigates the Mysteries of UFOs: Interstellar Travel, Crashes, and Government Cover-Ups*. Pompton Plains, NJ: New Page Books, 2008

Grace, N. B. *UFOs: What Scientists Say May Shock You!* (24/7: Science Behind the Scenes). New York, NY: Children's Press, 2008.

Kean, Leslie. *UFOs: Generals, Pilots and Government Officials Go on the Record*. New York, NY: Crown Publishing, 2010.

Kitei, Lynne D. *The Phoenix Lights: A Skeptic's Discovery That We Are Not Alone*. Newburyport, MA: Hampton Roads Publishing, 2010.

Marcel, Jesse, Jr., and Linda Marcel. *The Roswell Legacy: The Untold Story of the First Military Officer at the 1947 Crash Site*. Pompton Plains, NJ: New Page Books, 2008.

Randle, Kevin D. *Crash: When UFOs Fall from the Sky: A History of Famous Incidents, Conspiracies, and Cover-Ups.* Pompton Plains, NJ: Career Press, 2010.

Romanek, Stan. *Messages: The World's Most Documented Extraterrestrial Contact Story.* Woodbury, MN: Llewellyn Publications, 2009.

Stewart, Gail. *UFOs* (The Mysterious & Unknown). San Diego, CA: ReferencePoint Press, 2007.

Walker, Kathryn. *Mysteries of UFOs* (Unsolved!). New York, NY: Crabtree Publishing, 2008.

Walton, Travis. *Fire in the Sky: The Walton Experience.* New York, NY: Marlowe and Company, 1997.

Wells, H. G. *The War of the Worlds.* New York, NY: Tribeca Books, 2011.

Wencel, Dave. *UFOs* (The Unexplained). Minneapolis, MN: Bellwether Media, 2010.

Bibliography

Extraterrestrial Contact. "Selected UFO Cases." Retrieved February 18, 2011 (http://www.ufoevidence.org/cases/ufocaseshome.asp).

Extraterrestrial Contact. "UFO Topics." Retrieved February 18, 2011 (http://www.ufoevidence.org/topics/topicshome.asp).

Friedman, Stanton T. "Biography." Retrieved February 18, 2011 (http://www.stantonfriedman.com/index.php?ptp=stans_bio).

Friedman, Stanton T. *Captured! The Betty and Barney Hill UFO Experience: The True Story of the World's First Documented Alien Abduction.* Pompton Plains, NJ: New Page Books, 2007.

Friedman, Stanton T. *Flying Saucers and Science: A Scientist Investigates the Mysteries of UFOs: Interstellar Travel, Crashes, and Government Cover-Ups.* Pompton Plains, NJ: New Page Books, 2008.

Mutual UFO Network. "Famous UFO Cases." Retrieved February 18, 2011 (http://www.mufon.com/FamousUFOCases.html).

Randle, Kevin D. *Crash: When UFOs Fall from the Sky: A History of Famous Incidents, Conspiracies, and Cover-Ups.* Pompton Plains, NJ: Career Press, 2010.

University of Colorado. "Scientific Study of Unidentified Flying Objects (Condon Report)." Retrieved February 18, 2011 (http://files.ncas.org/condon).

Walton, Travis. "The Incident." Retrieved February 18, 2011 (http://www.travis-walton.com/ordinary.html).

Index

About the Author

Jennifer Bringle first became interested in UFOs as a kid when she saw *E. T.* In addition to this book, she's written nonfiction books for teens about everything from homelessness to hunting. She lives in North Carolina.

Photo Credits

Cover, p. 1 Shutterstock.com; cover, back cover, interior background image © www.istockphoto.com/Dusko Jovic; pp. 3, 6, 12, 24, 32 © www.istockphoto.com/Lee Pettet; pp. 4–5 Tim Boyle/Getty Images; p. 7 NOAA; p. 9 Chip Simons/Taxi/Getty Images; p. 13 © Columbia Pictures/Everett Collection; p. 15 © Mary Evans Picture Library/The Image Works; p. 17 U.S. Air Force/AFP/Getty Images; p. 22 © C.Walker/Topham/The Image Works; p. 25 © Mary Evans/Ronald Grant/Everett Collection; p. 27 Hulton Archive/Getty Images; p. 29 © AP Images; p. 33 Archive Photos/Getty Images; p. 34 © 20th Century Fox Film Corp/Everett Collection; p. 36 Getty Images.

Designer: Les Kanturek; Editor: Bethany Bryan; Photo Researcher: Amy Feinberg